STORYVILLE

Books by Linda France

Red (Bloodaxe Books, 1992)
Sixty Women Poets (Bloodaxe Books, 1993)
Acknowledged Land (Northumberland County Council, 1994)
The Gentleness of the Very Tall (Bloodaxe Books, 1994)
Storyville (Bloodaxe Books, 1997)

LINDA FRANCE

storyville

BLOODAXE BOOKS

ISBN: 1 85224 399 6

First published 1997 by
Bloodaxe Books Ltd,
P.O. Box 1SN,
Newcastle upon Tyne NE99 1SN.

Bloodaxe Books Ltd acknowledges
the financial assistance of Northern Arts.

Cover printing by J. Thomson Colour Printers Ltd, Glasgow.

Printed in Great Britain by
Cromwell Press Ltd, Broughton Gifford, Melksham, Wiltshire.

'If you kill a caribou, eat the fermented lichen in its stomach.'

S.A.S. SURVIVAL GUIDE

Acknowledgements

Acknowledgements are due to the editors of the following publications in which some of these poems first appeared: *Blade, Gairfish, Making for Planet Alice* (Bloodaxe Books, 1997), *Orbis, Plow/share, Scratch, Stand, Poetry Wales, The Tenth Muse* and *Writing Women*. Thanks are due to Marina Abramović for 'Role Exchange: A Found Poem'.

'Storyville' won joint first prize in the *Stand* Poetry Competition in 1996. 'Bruise' was overall winner in the Waterstones/Liverpool John Moores University Poetry Competition in 1996. 'Starfish' was first runner-up in the BBC Wildlife Poetry Competition in 1995. 'Pillow Talk' was commissioned by BBC 1's *Bookworm* and 'Polo at Windsor' by BBC 2's *On the Line* in 1994. 'The Wall' was commissioned for Huddersfield Contemporary Music Festival's celebration of the work of Wolfgang Rihm in 1995. 'Home Movies' and 'Interior Fictions' were written to accompany an exhibition of photographs, also called *Interior Fictions*, by John Askew. 'The Nine Muses' formed part of a collaboration with photographer Karen Melvin for the 1995 Hexham Abbey Festival.

The first section of this book, 'Storyville', is a part of a collaboration with artist Birtley Aris, with accompanying original music by Keith Morris and Lewis Watson, premièred at the Queen's Hall Arts Centre, Hexham, in April 1997. The cover of this book shows a detail from one of Birtley Aris's paintings. The section emblems are also by Birtley Aris.

Linda France wishes to thank Northern Arts for a Writer's Award given in 1995.

Contents

STORYVILLE

Mess With It

'If you don't know what jazz is, don't mess with it.'
FATS WALLER

It creeps up behind you on all fours,
a reed between its teeth, so quiet
you barely notice. Until it's too late:
smoky breath tickles your neck keening
its sweetness and you toss back your head
in red surrender. The blood beneath your skin
runs hot as sex, cold as death. You borrow
its velvet pelt, watching your face lost
in the mirror of its Spanish eyes.
If you have to ask what it is,
you'll probably never know.

It's a secret for anyone with ears,
an inkling to dance like an oyster
with a black pearl heart. The sea
isn't deep enough for its blue.
It swims you till your lips are salt
and crazy. Never was an ache more
beautiful; like the love you fall into
too easy. If you don't know what it is,
don't mess with it.

It will score your belly with gorgeous claws,
tug your guts into tight cords.
You'll lose yourself in its glorious bite
and no one will believe the height
of your eyes. It will love you then leave you
with just a brush of silver on the rim
of your high-hat. And when the sun goes down
you'll catch yourself swaying to the fragrance
of sweating lilies, blowing their white horns
as if there was no tomorrow.
There isn't. You know what it is.
Love it while it lasts. Mess with it.

The Devil's Music

High days and holidays we play
the devil's tunes, fill the heavens
with do you wanna hear, do you wanna hear
Ragtime, Dixie. Bud collects race records –
shining black, restricted, fragile.

Down here we don't go about hitting
too many white keys. And it doesn't matter,
nothing really matters when we flash
our brass and syncopate right in the eye
of the sun, like a swarm of mayflies

sighing across the waters. We're Arkansas
Travellers and Turkeys in the Straw.
Bud says the thing about jazz is
you can't lie; you play from the heart.
And folk listening hear it through their feet.

The girls kick off their shoe leather
and the dust rises up like the dead.
We know how to put the blues to bed;
this music, the only thing we're slaves to.
The devil's own horn, that sassy trombone,

Lordy Lordy double bass, those big
fat drums, cool as cool cool water
clarinet and the cotton-picking banjo –
our instruments of war,
our terrible, sweet revenge.

Kansas City

On a quiet one off the main drag,
it's dark outside the rinky-dink De Luxe –
a wired indigo of twinklers, shadows

that might be driftsmoke if only
Old Fireball was cutting some rug.
The slammer is shut like a kisser

that doesn't dig liquor any day
of the week. It's fish-black unlucky,
hawk's out with his axe; but we know

when we fall in there'll be scumpteen fish
to blow our lids, glistening scales and hot pepper,
some solid juice to wash it down.

We've been saving our rocks all week.
Let's hit that belly-chord. Shake out your vine
and shimmy like a foxy fish.

52nd Street

The black cars are crackling like a wireless
in the rain, shining like the sweat

on a black man's cheeks as he plays
the trumpet sweeter than an angel. Neon

is hot as chilli, spiking your tongue,
tempting you in whichever joint

is jumping highest. It only costs
a dollar to step down into the cellar

where soon you'll be touching the sky. All
the shadows will be your friends. The music

fingers, plucks and blows the dark away –
brass, ivory, sycamore, skin – a glass

in your hand, a foot that won't stop tapping.

Blues for Bird

What you did to the blues
was the sound of a bird
trapped behind broken glass
beating at the liquid
light, struggling to fly free.
You crushed bones with your horn.

They all told you a horn
shouldn't be blown that free
and fast. You played the blues
hot as neon, liquid
gas. Your sax and a glass
of booze – you were a bird.

And they called you *Yard bird*
too, singing back home blues
twitching that brassy horn
full of amber liquid –
those notes that shone like glass
made you dream you were free.

Say who of us is free?
We all live under glass
wishing we were bird,
sky gold with angel horn.
But we swim in the blues –
indigo, turquoise, liquid

as the sea. Your liquid
cocktail was spiked with horn
of horse. Nothing is free.
On the streets, doing bird
they followed you, those blues –
tears just mirrors of glass.

But still you'd fill your glass,
pick up, polish your horn.
The tune spilled like liquid
from your lips. You were free
as death – your soul a bird.
You earned your breath, your blues.

Bird, you're a ghost of glass,
liquid mid all those blues –
free at last, your horn, you.

Round Midnight

Round about midnight
all your sins rise up to heaven
like rings of smoke.

Your body's aching,
a devil with two horns
who wants no trouble.

That lonely heart soars
through blue, misses
a couple of beats.

A lullaby ripple is
dreaming another day
round about midnight.

The Snake's Hips and the Clam's Garter

'What we play is life.'

LOUIS ARMSTRONG

They're all hands, every riff another fingertip,
snoozing the nap of velvet, schmoozing sand and stones
till they swing, while Oscar unlocks that piano
as if he held the key to your body, could read
the blue notes of your dreams. Listen. *Ella. Louis.*
The nearness of you.

Summer breeze, meadow lark, moonlight: the best tunes,
the most beautiful words in the world. You're there,
glowing, when the trumpet stretches out like a shadow,
your own shadow, whispering in the silver dark.
She's a honeysuckle rose, trickling nectar,
and he's a bee

who thinks he's a tiger, drunk on cognac in April
in Paris. And you know they're stealing the show
just for you, turning the words on like lamps in fog,
under a blanket of blue, enjoying the rhymes
like a bird enjoys the sky, high as tomorrow's sun.
Tenderly.

Every day's a lovely day and Louis's a birthday boy,
all tie and tux and a tongue he can't keep from
tooting, a voice he can't stop smiling. Cheek to cheek.
And Ella is how many candle flames it takes
to burn you. Not hurt you. Together they scat
one hell of a *yes.*

Storyville

'The word jazz, originally jass, was a New Orleans word for sexual intercourse. The connection between the music and the sexual activity is that jazz emerged in the brothels of Storyville in New Orleans, where musicians were employed to entertain, and perhaps to stimulate, the clientele waiting their turn to enjoy what they had come for.'
BREWER'S TWENTIETH CENTURY PHRASE AND FABLE

Whatever else I can say about you,
you were the first. You wrote your name all over
me. You had me against a wall. You took
your shirt off in Harlem and no one jeered.

I hitched a ride to the Cotton Club
on the back of your motor-bike. The fur
collar of your leather jacket tickled
my nose. In all my photos you're smiling

like a parrot and I'm just a feather.
When I said *Take Five* you blew your own trumpet,
roared off; the stunt man's big scene. You crashed.
I was a witness. As a gesture, frankly,

it didn't work. Fifteen years later, I met
a dog, your name in silver under its chin.

*

You were too tall for me, my mad giraffe.
I was forever kissing the tops
of your thighs, their jungly safari skin.

Sometimes you'd kneel down gently, as only
giants can, to tell me how clouds fillet
mackerel skies. You said you had to hang
your tears out to dry. I knitted a ladder

of wool to pull over your eyes. We danced,
me astraddle the saddle of your spine.
We were circus, trapeze, without a net.
My smile was sequins. But I cried rhinestones
out in the T-bird when you said your mind was on
higher things – telegraph poles and pylons.

When I'm flying my kite, I think of you.

*

Last night I dreamt about my April Fool
again. His eyes full as a gazelle's,
he gathered me into their wild dark.
Stroking my petals, he called me *Flower*.

We were flying to New York and I left
behind a boy in yellow shoes playing
a three-stringed double bass. Its frets were ocean
in my ears. My April Fish landed

belly-up and though I tickled him till
my nails bled, the life had gone from his mouth,
those hungry lips I fed with kisses, beer
and pretzels. I wrapped the sadness of him

in a map of Europe, laid him beneath
my pillow so I'd dream of tulips and eggs.

*

You played the hookah like Charlie Parker
in the shower, wearing your hat from Tibet.

You came at me like a crab, sideways, rolling
your crustacean eyes. Together we cracked

your shell and our breath streamed orange. We swam
in canals, gobbling the raw herring

of our hearts. We stayed up all night, listening
to be-bop on the radio, gleaming

brass crowbars into saxophones we'd blow
till our mouths were raw as our stinging eyes,

weeping with love's sweet anarchy. *Come
the revolution, love*, you said. *Let's dance.*

We shimmied on the sloping rooftops and
caught the stars as they bounced off the water.

*

For a whole month all we ate was honey.
We were drunk as bees, combing each other
out of wax, like drones. A rainbow littered
our bed with horns of gold and we planted

a euphonium hedge. All that wax melted
and trickled, covered us with a second skin.
Didn't the Messiah come from New Orleans
to share our bed? We made offerings

of sourmash and signed our names. I lifted
my head and sang about skillets, shortnin' bread.
Until the coal man with laughing eyes moused

his way inside our hive. We had plenty
of coal but all our mirrors were broken.
That whole life went up in crimson creole flames.

*

Whatever else I can say about you,
you were the first; the blue note of your voice –
elderberry, malt, moonshine. I didn't
stand a chance. Your vices were my vices.

Your voice was the voice I wanted to speak
to me. For old times' sake we visited
the zoo and you were the most dangerous
animal. That night, fireworks slashed the sky

over Birdland. Bessie danced in her grave
and all our friends died. We went to dig up
old men's bones. Whatever else I can say
about you, you always get me drunk.

It's not a problem while the cellar's full;
but I'll drink you dry as death and taxes.

*

He thought he was a high-flier, wanted
me to chart him a map of the stars.
I didn't know which way was North; the needle

pricked my finger. His bloodshot eyes were
a camera and I made wings of my arms,
whispering *Alpha, Bravo, Charlie* in

the fuzz box of his left ear. As we slept,
someone called through the skin of the wall
Goodnight, Aeroplane. My silk dressing-gown

was the colour of mangrove swamps. But south
of the bayou, his house was torched. The heat
singed my tail. Sometimes, by accident,

we collided at the station, and were grounded,
while the tannoy warned travellers of fire.

*

You were the one who took me out West
and – I think it's true – forgot to bring
me back. Your house was a raku cave

and I was Monterey Jack. We got
stranded on that desert island, palm trees
swaying, Billie singing; jalapeno
peppers stung my lips but everything
was cool as the ice we crushed into
our mint juleps. You were neon, dammit.
You sent me scuttling for cover, a rabbit
out on the prairie; even though the moon
on your left breast made me feel like a bad girl,
with bats setting up home in my belfry.

Don't hate me – I'm just a baby who loves jazz.

*

If you were a drum, I'd play you with brushes
of silver wire, kissing your cymbals

every fourth beat, until your world spun
with a thousand suns. When you're a guitar,

you switch on the shocking north and south
of your electric mouth. Sing me some scat,

sweetheart, and I'll take care of the rhythm boys.
I want to lead the orchestra

of your body so you stand and deliver
an encore. Solo. Our mad moods leave

us indigo but Saturday nights
we'll always step out, wearing each other's clothes,

and sway to someone else's beat we'll call
our own, footprints in chalk on the dance floor.

*

And when it was all over, it happened
again. A small spore fell from the Planet
Jazz and planted itself in the tense place
at the back of her neck, the soft spot
she had for the fingers of guitarists.

The whistle blew and the A-Train took her
to Kansas City where they played games
like owls that ended by morning. His beard
hid stricken lips, whispering words of filth.

All of them rhymed. She confessed her pelvis
had suddenly turned into the larynx
of Ella Fitzgerald. All the windows
were shattered. She sent postcards to his hands,
scented with vanilla, Coney Island.

*

I made a mistake. It happens. No regrets.
I spoke to you as if you were the moon.

And you aren't and it isn't made of cheese;
nor is it a film with a soundtrack by
Courtney Pine. It's a hare on a white plate.

Look. That summer I wanted to box
with you on the sidewalk but you were jumpy
as an eggplant waiting to be fried
in batter. The crescent moon sang *Swing! Swing!*

I know your sort. All talk. Sideshow
you're not. I juggle three full moons, learning
how to let them fall − a lady singing
the blues about the heat in her blood,
the colour of a coward she could've loved.

*

This is the book of the film – *Storyville*.

I'm sitting here, smoking, waiting
for the world to catch on fire, to match
the furnace in my heart. Someone else
will have to write the words; I'll be too busy
striking chords in a good man's eyes;
his baby grand beneath a spinning ball
of mirrors. And I never kiss and tell.
Unless I'm paid good money. Never trust
a girl who only knows the tune of her own
secrets. This is everybody's story.

And jazz is the wild card you play through
the night while all your aces are still
better up your sleeve than on the table.

*

HOME MOVIES

Home Movies

I *Fast forward*

What he chooses to remember
is sad as acid. It's all inside and
he's still just a small boy
sitting on dewy grass,
chewing on a hunk of bread,
lips greased with butter.
He says it's beautiful:
it happens to music like memory,
like a stopped clock on a mantelpiece
where it's always tea-time
and rungs of chairs a ladder reaching
tomorrow. The wallpaper will be endless
summer. Seen through a window,
everything he dreams is angles:
the ache in his belly,
the shadows, the lids of his eyes.
Elephants come to question
how is it to live indoors,
what chooses to be remembered.

II *Rewind*

What chooses to be remembered?
How is it to live indoors?
Elephants come to question
the shadows, the lids of his eyes,
the ache in his belly.
Everything he dreams is angles,
summer seen through a window.
Tomorrow the wallpaper will be endless
and rungs of chairs a ladder reaching
where it's always tea-time,
like a stopped clock on a mantelpiece.
It happens to music like memory.
He says it's beautiful.
Lips greased with butter,
chewing on a hunk of bread,
sitting on dewy grass,
he's still just a small boy;
is sad as acid. It's all inside and
what he chooses to remember.

Making Sense

1 *The Smell of It*

prickled the inside of my nose, tickled
my throat with toxic fingers. Vast open vats
of yellow and blue, churning round and round
into their own colour. And butter,
school jumpers, custard, all the doors
we ever had. Blue Riband wafers. They were
Cuisinaire colours. Magic. And my father
uttered the holy words: *Swarfega. Paypacket. Bait.*

I balanced on the industrial scale,
clocking up the numbers, me and a ridged drum,
envying its heavy presence, the fact
of its bright future: CLODOL stencilled
on its side in gold like a broken code.

In the mess room Baby Belling was neat
and fat with sausage rolls, tea in cracked mugs
before a hand of brag or rummy, cards hot
and speckled as eggs. Behind the door hung
a calendar I wasn't meant to see
through the thick smoke that stung like a blister
over the smell of paint: my father's smell,
ochrish and peacock, the suck of tin lids.

My mouth is a dream of how nothing should be:
faces too close to mine, greasy as sausages;
something green; the flash of dripping knives and forks;
the taint of gas, phenol-thick, pink candy-floss.

And always my mouth stretched open as I hurtle
in and out of the cartoon café. They tell me off
for screaming. I can taste red metal at the back
of my throat. I swallow the duck-billed numbness.

Let my legs platypus me home. Pollen
of heliotrope, its antiseptic tang
still clinging to my webbed tongue, I hold on to
my mother's hand; keep her where I can see her.

Back in the safe glades of kitchen country,
dinner is a prize for being bingo brave:
a Cornish pasty nestled and shiny
on its plate in a billow of horse's breath.

I can taste the smell of it; attack it with
my stainless steel. But my mouth doesn't know what
to do; it's forgotten how to chew. The *thought*
of eating hurts. My best pasty, my St Michael

Cheesy Puffs will not pass my lips. Instead
I must sip homeopathic cream of tomato,
feed the taste of blood with the taste of blood
and wait for my teeth to grow back, wolvish, vengeful.

3 *The Touch of It*

was the braille of my beginning, telling
me how the same thing could be different:

my mother's, in the distance, soft, freckled
and capable; my father's, tough, brambled,

smelling of sun and factories, stale beer.
Summer, the house was full of it, gritty

with salt and sand. Mam rubbed my skin so hard
it hurt, the towel scratching my goosebumps

away. Dad pretended not to notice
he was stroking my bare feet like they were

puppy's ears; then he'd make a meal of my toes
till I squealed. My fingers followed the map

of the shrapnel craters on his broad back;
the picture of a rose on his arm, thorned

with black hairs; the curls he kept in his vest.
My mother's skin was a secret I'd soon

find in the stretch of my own tingling flesh.
Something to do with their wedding photo,

moody and matte. And something else it could
never catch: the touch of their workers' hands

branding me with an itch for serious play.

Home always started with *E*.
You stuck your chin out and enjoyed it,
lips stretched in a smile.
You had fun with *yer bugs*
when no one was listening; knew it had nothing
to do with insects. You could spit a bit
and pretend it was a mistake.

This was our secret, black and white,
the magpie music that made my house home.
No other child I knew was called *Woman man*.
I was everything I wanted to be.

Night was the coal settling in the grate;
no one talking because *Steptoe* was on,
The Fugitive, Till Death Us Do Part.
Until the *Nine O'Clock News*, when it was
all *Eee, yer bugs*, tickles and cups of milky tea.

That was before I went to the Grammar School
where they taught me not to speak with my mouth open.

I want it back, that clash of lips and teeth
and spit. I chase your ghosts up Grainger Street,
down Gallowgate; hear the sound of myself
listening, like a foreigner, reading lips;
feel the grin in my gut when my children say *bath*.

5 *The Sight of It*

was what happened when you were dreaming
and didn't close your eyes:
upstairs was a pink ship, drifting far out to sea
on waves of pirate sunlight. Flowers grew
in neat rows on the high sides. You counted them
and tried to catch the motes of dust in the air.

You chased them down the wooden hill
into the dark corners of doorframe and skirting,
the curl of cold lino. Downstairs was always
cold, the forest of tables and chairs where

Mother's Pride and *Daddies* taught you to read,
where metal flew at you and made scarlet,
where doors snapped shut like the end of books,
where medicine was thick and liquorice.

Try as you might you can't see the soft shape
a body makes swimming under water.

You're too busy fighting for breath, struggling
to crack the code that will tell you what
those words mean: *Daddies, Mother's Pride.*

But when you've grown big enough to reach
the latch, to open the door, your face
is flooded with the yellow of butter,

the word you know means something else,
a word shedding its sense, like *light.*

My Mother, the Sea

Let me tell you a secret about
my mother. She was a mermaid who wore
lipstick, bloody as sea anemones
underwater. She sat all day on a rock
combing her naturally auburn hair
and never had to go to work. She knew
where all the treasure chests lay buried
so she didn't give a whelk about money.

Because she was a mermaid she made
children in secret, with no pain; sent them
to school with the fishes, taught them how to
eat oysters in any month with a moon
to row them home. She was courted by Neptune
and Hollywood but much preferred knitting.
O her nets were the talk of the ocean!
Fine as spray and spindrift, flossed with fine pearls.

And I'm proud to be one of her daughters –
the way I swim so strong, length by length
the City Pool. My breaststroke's the envy
of dolphins. The scales of my skin match
her own. But now she's gone full fathom five
all I have left are her stories I knit
into patterns like wide blue waves I dive
into, never once coming up for air.

The Meat Factory

The smell of raw meat is Chanel No.5.
It feels as if I'm right at home here
among the viscera, the flesh made new
and candy pink.
                    Dressed in disinfectant blue,
wellingtons, caps and rubber gloves, everyone
squelches on the tiled floor, stripping the willow
of troughs of offal to the dying chords
of the slaughterhouse next door.
                    Eggs are slotted
into the sockets of blushing, marbled pies.
Sausages are sleeved into cuff-linked lines.
Antique machines prick pat-a-cake pies,
six at a time for my baby and me.

Like summer rain, blood is never very far
away, the colour of the heart, the lights,
the sweet sweet breads.
                    Let me tell you, I've got the glad eye
for the boss of the chicken room, snowy with feathers
that tickle your gizzard, women cackling,
their fingers plucking. My skin is savoury
bumps.
                    Lunchtimes we go upstairs to the canteen,
carnal with smoke and greasy newsprint, and eat
anything at all with gravy, counting
the notes in our paypackets, already
twistin' the gnawed bone of Friday night away.

Waiting with My Yellow Dog

The woman who sleeps all day
makes origami birds
out of toffee wrappers.

Her neighbour's zimmer
kicks its rubber hooves, dreaming
of gentle jockeys with white hair.

My ears, powerful as whelks,
practise listening moistly,
like a slug, trailing silver.

I cool the air in the tomb
of my lips with glyphs of gold,
mistrals whispering at the doors,

windows hooked with flamingo beaks.
A yellow dog sits at my side,
drinking all my sins. We are twins,

nameless, faithful, Siamese.
Night surrenders into day
with the charm of real birds

in an imaginary garden,
fine as the cracks in my bones.
Hot flanks twitching, my bed hacks

towards dawn. The starched sheets
stripe me sore in the saddle.
The nurses' shoes sing me

a lullaby in morse;
hands stroke me like owls, dapple
me like mares, fluff my pillows

into the bellies of bears.
All night long I lie there
just waiting for my hair to turn white.

Her Dogness

Life as we knew it has come to an end
since you arrived, puking on our shoulders
in the car. Now, things get done with you

chewing our shoelaces, ankles, the dip
of my best frock, whatever you can get
your teeth into. So who wants to keep

a tidy house when there's the pink of your belly
to be tickled? The speckled thrush
of your muzzle to be nuzzled and stroked?

The irrepressible wag of your white-
tipped tail to lift the corners of my mouth?
All I want is a collie dog to walk with

across the fell, watching the wind
ripple across her back like a dark field
of wheat. Your tongue comes undone like a belt.

My nose is wet. But best is when we come
home and stretch out in front of the fire, two
mad and muddy humbugs who are getting

to know the sound of each other's snores;
two legs and four legs, dreaming of more legs.

Starfish

He said it was a gift.
And she took it. Even though

its fingers reached beyond her own.
She clasped its centre in her palm

like the hand of a stranger, till it shed
grains of sand, and she felt like low-tide.

After he'd gone she was
a beachcomber, smelling the history

of sea, a recipe for fish
fermented into cheese. The star

in its underbelly made a man, open
as ocean, intricate as an ancient insect.

She told its five points, surely
not only echinoderm: they were

sky and snake, thigh, sword and gate.
This creature should never have died.

The sea would always miss it.
Those five carbuncled limbs

were columns, all pointing to Rome,
which, like her, would burn.

Sabbath

The moon was the body of god
on the tongue of the shriven sky
when you purred and told me,
wet or dry, I had the best pelt
this side of Dolphin's Barn.
You frilled the squirrel of me
wide open. And I was blessed.
Mountain air pressed my flesh
as if it were water we swam in,
bubbling with peaty secrets.
Then all you uttered, ruttish
as a fox, was *Shush now. Glory.*
Mist stained the yellow leaves
like glass, a hundred hands opening
and closing. A single trunk
felled in the forest. The sound
of it was thunder. The smell of it
was bog and bracken and beeswax.
I vowed I'd never forget it.
The harvest night you ottered me.

Intertextual

Come, curl up in skeins of narrative,
print our palms with patterns like Belgian lace,
breathe in that virgin ink and paper over
and over. Sweetheart, aren't we book-lovers?

As our pages turn, we'll read the rhythms
in the deckle of each other's eyes. Seduced
by what words can do, we'll whisper *good*
and *beautiful* in the weave of ears, feel

our fingers trace their strange braille, fluent grammar,
the comfort of bindings, the dangerous
certainty of authorship. We'll exchange
slim volumes to lip and tongue, learn each other

by heart. Don't we collect first editions, love?
Aren't our walls striped like tigers? Between
the covers, let's scribble in the margins,
write our names on each other's spines, *The Complete Works*.

Pillow Talk

I am the keeper of your dreams,
that white horizon, the cut cord.

I am cradle, cot and playground,
a fairy-tale of wolves and wishes.

A third of your life you'll give to me.
Come, lie naked between my sheets.

Aren't I an expert in sweat and secrets,
your body's lost-and-found,

its best three-letter word?
I'll be roses and daisies forever.

And ever. Rest in me.

Bruise

When you borrowed my jacket, like a pirate
borrows gold, you sniffed its empty arm

as if it were a rose and said it smelled
of me. *Parma violets.* That's how we laughed,

mauve and crackling; the sweet taste of each other
in our stained mouths, painting our names

a new colour. I wore your palomino shoes
but they pinched my toes. On the dance floor

we couldn't see for sequins. The silver light
made masks of our faces, guarding the drama

our lips had no words for. You took to
cruising around town, wearing my jacket

like a totem, a flayed skin. We were flowers
with heart-shaped leaves thriving on disturbed ground.

I tried to give up the violets
on the white insides of my wrists,

the cords of my neck; cut my hair and dipped
my aching body in vanilla, musk.

Why is it we always miss each other now
when we call? That when I think of you

a ghost of a bruise blooms behind my eyes,
something sweet seeds the air but doesn't root?

Essential Oils

I walk through a perfectly ordinary door,
welcomed by you in your little white *Trust me* coat,
the lingering fragrance of oils, lemongrass,

lavender, a padded cocoon of silence.
Either side of a starburst, we sit and talk
as you decide which bottles to open, let drops

fall into the petalled Chinese bowl. Even this
feels like a gift. Discreetly you leave the room
for enough time it takes to slip off my clothes,

scale the high couch and lie down, my face emptying
itself in the moon-shaped space. Then you press *Play*
and the room is liquid with bells and pianos.

Your hands start at the sacrum and flow up-river.
My muscles melting, I'm liquid too. Your fingers
walk through the ridges of my spine. It tickles

and I'm laughing at your feathers that give me wings.
You rub me with bergamot, chamomile and grapefruit
until my black and blue is all red. There is nothing

but this – my body in your hands, the matching
rhythms of our breathing. You knead me like dough
that will rise and rise, drawing the meridians

in my thighs, stretching my neck to perfection,
picking up all the stitches I've dropped, until I feel
like Fatima's mother-in-law, a woman

with no enemies. Or Captain Cook stroked back
to the land of No Sciatica by
the miraculous hands of twelve skilled women

from Tahiti. The sun is shining inside me.
I'm back on course; your gift, the thirty roses
it takes to make one single drop of essential oil.

At the Moulin de la Galette

(after Renoir)

I want to be that woman whose smile
is like the sun, a gift of flowers
in her lap, her friend's hand on her shoulder.

I want to be the man whose body leans
towards her in a gesture of longing
she answers back with her eyes.

I want to be the party girl, all flirt
and banter, the man whispering a secret
in his partner's ear, the mother teasing

her daughter, the gentleman smoking
his pipe in silence. All of them are dappled
and laughter, Sunday and polka.

The lights are moons of glass drawing the tides
of everyone's hats. The music's breeze
and brass make my feet itch.

I want to be there, in Paris, in summer.
Let's rattle the gates, step into the garden,
drink Kir Royale, take each other's hands and dance.

Solveig's Song

I sing as I sew, stitching up the home's hearth
into the weeping white rings of onions.

I've read and read my prayerbook till it's thin
as skin. The distance between us is hide;

that buck who dragged you across continents
of snow. Away from me. Here I stay

keeping company with snow's sister,
the moon, with my silver needle; our patchwork

honeymoon quilt growing and growing, broad
as antlers in springtime, our feathered bed.

My father was right. Don't think I'm still
your snowball girl, Peer Gynt: a good no

is better than a bad yes. In your absence,
I sing songs that summon wolves, the red eyes

of trolls. I bleed the colours of schnapps,
spin yarns you've never heard the like of. Egypt

and deserts and their dancing girls
are buttons I sew on so tight they'll never fall off.

If you came home now, I'd beat you with birches,
spiny as antlers; make you feel the sting of that onion,

the moon. Don't you know you're a bastard stag,
a rotten, rotten onion?

Self Portrait

It was autumn. All I could do.
Every morning the milky light
lapping at my window. I rose

from the desert of my bed, clicked
on Brahms, Schubert or something else
Germanic; sipped orange juice while

I found my brush, a square I could
fit my face on. For forty-two
days I looked at my lips, my eyes,

their arrangement within the shape
of brow, jaw; sometimes triangle,
sometimes oval. Always hounded,

hungry, abandoned. My poor face.
I discovered it didn't quite look
how I thought. Old. Blond. Glasses.

And I'm still the boy who cycled home
to find his father sitting
in an armchair outside the phone-box.

I'm still surprised. The white canvas
welcomed me in like a bed.
And I charted my features

like a desert, like pillows, like a dog
waiting to be fed. Every day
for six weeks I painted myself

coming out of the dark tunnel
of myself, the cool oasis
of forty-two faces.

Polyphemus and Galatea

(after Odilon Redon)

He looks at her as he loves her,
with the tenderness of the wounded.
As if she were treasure he'd found
in a cave – sapphires, emeralds, amber,
the jewels of her flesh, sleeping.
All looking and no touching,

he's sated with the taste of desire;
but saved from the sadness of having.
His single eye drifts over her
like a moon, its amethyst shadow
bruising the horizon. His one eye.
A single tear. His left hand steadies

the hillside, a door he'll never open.
One kiss would kindle an earthquake.
Stroking her breasts, he'd crush her
like a grape. The love in his look
belongs to a child. One lost in another room.
Locked in his enormous eye. Howling.

The Nine Muses

'There is a vitality, a life force, an energy, a quickening, that is translated through you into action, and because there is only one of you in all time, this expression is unique. And if you block it, it will never exist through any other medium and will be lost.'

MARTHA GRAHAM

I

Your body will always bring you back
to yourself: the limits of your skin,

your senses, you know are doors that can
open or close. The key is tucked in

the pocket of your heart. Its silver
shines when you start to sing and your toes

tap a tattoo on stone. Your arms build
an arch, an angel's wings. For soaring.

Your tongue is a flame burning your mouth.

II

Your tongue is a flame burning your mouth
with your mother's memory of war,

swords flashing their mirrors in men's eyes –
a litany of battles (*place, date,*

how many fallen); the children whose
bellies ache, whose wounds nobody heals.

This door has a lock you need to pick;
all your muscle, your cunning, to blow

your breath through the cracks where light trickles.

III

Your breath through the cracks where light trickles
is how dawn begins: ten fingers stroke

the margins of sky and the sleeping
snake of horizons; turn into two

hands, palming the land into waking.
Or how a heart of rock is softened

by the salt of tears, the wind of clocks
ticking, corners broken by knowing

change happens, like a door opening.

IV

Change happens like a door opening,
and then what music spills from the sky

to slake the dry of voices too long
silent, striving to echo liquid.

A flute is playing like a story
you heard as a child, or told yourself

in dreams. The story is a ribbon
in your hair, curling round a mountain.

Your body is flute, flower and root.

V

Your body is flute, flower and root
as the keys of your silk open and

open, your corolla thrilling with
what love brings, the seeds of its magic.

You sing hymns to columbine, tulip,
rose; and the world and his wife love you,

breathing the spores of your wild-garden,
fists unfurling in the mulch, the milk;

your surrender, your moon of a mouth.

VI

Your surrender, your moon of a mouth –
what else is to be said but *circus*,

clown, trapeze. The colours own no words
but themselves. The blind lead the blind through

a hall of mirrors and emerge creased
up laughing. The shapes of their bodies

are physicks, questions of faith, jokes played
on horses jumping through hoops of fire;

always the danger of being singed.

VII

Always the danger of being singed
isn't any reason not to soar,

not to let the mask fall. The drama's
in the letting go; diving into

flight. What feels like height is improvised;
an accident you'll practise every

time you melt, crash; learning once again
how to tumble with grace, remember

the architecture of light, the stars.

VIII

The architecture of light, the stars
are not ceiling or slate. We spin it

with those arrows that shoot from our eyes
when dark is our only answer. Then

we are most blessed. The stars rest like crowns
on our heads. And the moon turns the tide

of our waters, drips its wax along
the length of our changes: how long to

travel from heaven to earth. And back.

IX

Travel from heaven to earth and back
and you will notice you are dancing

the steps of a spiral, a willow stripped
and woven. What you are is a tree

you must cast yourself, into its own
mould: embroider with leaves, blossom, fruit;

flirt with the birds and the breeze. Know this
is flesh, the gift of your muse – the map of

your body will always bring you back.

Riverwise

'The health of the salmon to you – a long life and a wet mouth.'
IRISH TOAST

What else do you want, or need, to be
but free, to live life in three dimensions,
where the waters are cool and clean, flow
from their source to the sea, sky a circle
of light above your head?

What else is more
beautiful than this liquid weightlessness,
that natural talent for leaping
out of your element and into air?

Guard the memory of your journey
in your chambered heart; remember what it is
to make redd, be egg, parr or smolt.
Swim or be still for days on end.
Navigate by the sun and the stars; smell
your way home in the dark.

Honour the river
you belong to, as it belongs to you,
its shrimps and sand eels, herrings and sprats.
You are its colour, shell and silver,
its blood and bone.

What else could you wish for
but the salmon's wisdom: the staying,
the setting-out and the returning;
like the fizz of bubbles in water,
the spawning of the new?

The Wall

Everyone says the wall is made of stone.
Thicker than a man lying down to sleep,

as long as a country is wide, it snakes the scarp
of the land. How many hands were skinned

in building it? How many years scarred? Every day
dawn treads barefoot, birdless across the grass

and dresses the wall in its secret greys,
lichen mapping each rock with false borders.

I see now the wall was built stone by stone
from silence. The wordlessness of pain.

In this place it always rains, wind washing
wet into the weather of the wall who can see

over, who can cross? Everyone forgets silence
can be broken, like an egg, spilling its gold,

walls fall with a single word. Here no birds sing.
And nobody is talking to nobody else.

Polo at Windsor

This is the ritual. This is the game.
There are many rules. The sun will shine.
All thoroughbreds are equal, some more
equal than others. You will be well-trained,
well-groomed. You must always look your best.
Toss your head and snort a stream of gorgeous
vowels. You may not be awfully bright,
but what you've got is class, the sheen
of sterling across your silken flanks.

You will be fed and watered at someone
else's expense on the close-clipped lawn,
till you feel the adrenalin course
through your veins, like Pimms, like champagne,
the muddy sapphire of blood. Bare your teeth,
coast, thunder, twist, foul. Darling, your life's
at stake. How many minutes of glory
while the shutters whirr, the mallets click?
Main player, you won't be ridden roughshod.

And if you're lucky, if you're a winner,
the Queen of England will stroke you
with her gloved hand. You can take home
a Cartier bauble with your aching legs,
your splitting head. Don't fret if you're hot
and steamy at the end of the day;
there'll always be someone to put you back
in your box, strip you off and bed you down.
That is the ritual. That is the game.

The Organist Entertains

I take it all back.
Everything I said about organs.
Now I sing a different tune.
With pistons.

O organ, how I love
the way your pipes,
like silver cadillacs,
move me; make me
spin like candy floss,
a carousel horse,
sky circling my belly.

Funny, how you laugh
as you scale my octaves,
startle me with just one
note. Opening and closing
like a fan, you tease the air.

Reginald, let down your hair
and toss your head
like a phantom
as the lights go down.

Aren't I a heroine in black
and white, flanked by crimson
velvet? And won't the baddie
meet his maker, as I tumble into
the crescendo of your arms,
out of danger?

Don't even think of playing
Here Comes the Bride.
Just keep on pulling out all
the stops and I'll set fire
to your sheet music.

Chip City

The train that carried me there was a chip,
crunching along tracks made of chips.
When I got off, the streets were paved with chips,
crisp and golden. There were vertical chips
for streetlights, sprinkling a salty glow at night
when newspapers flew in the spaces between chips
and roosted, rustling their greasy wings.
The people were chips with clothes on,
pushing chips on wheels, walking chips on leads,
chips that cried and barked. They knew they were all chips
off the old block and they'd never drive turbo chips,
never live in semi-detached chips;
they'd never have a body like a french fry
however hard they tried to make the fat fly.
And for this they all had chips
on their shoulders, soused in vinegar.
And why not when there was nothing but chips,
wrapped or open, the only word on everyone's lips,
larding the city's wriggling hips,
drifting out to sea like the ghost of fish and ships?

Fair City

After dark the DART rolls its metal
past our window like a clock chiming.
The half moon of my buttock shines its silver
on your showered thigh; my belly tucks in
your hip. Your lips feather my open beak,
tickling me into a dream of a woman
singing, her breasts salty as cockles.
I sleep to the racket of her engine.

Until I collide with silence, crashing
me awake to the smell of sweat tattooing
my skin; last night's bar sawdust in my mouth;
rusty streetlights spidering the ceiling.
I trace the arc of your arm over me:
its weight holding me in like a gate
I can lean over and look beyond
but have no desire to open.

The air crows its coolness across my face.
The traffic's back, the DART. We're citizens
of flesh, breathing in the morning's fresh greys.
Let me brush you with the rise
of a pigeon's wing; kiss you with the soft hunger
of a limbo dancer on Grafton Street
so we'll wake breaking the bread of our bodies
into buttery crumbs, strawberry jam.

Still Life

What you do to me is tulips,
a most exquisite invention,
six perfect petals, the colour
of May, of might, of between seasons.
They breathe the just-washed scent of you,
peeling off your petals, brushing

against the new spring of my skin,
the silk of yours my fingers lift
and release like the pour of morning.
How many senses does a flower,
or someone sharing a room
with tulips, need? See how their leaves

are lazy but proud; their cups, filling
with heat, bold and opening,
spill shocks of white, dusty purple,
the sound of you entering me
like the earth who made you, tulips,
gorgeous, elegant, heavy with wanting

only to be themselves, their curve
and searching. Always bring me tulips:
their mad dancing of hidden words,
their calligraphy of secrets:
bed; come; their stretch of corolla
around a dark ring of rising,

of rightness I just get lost in
and find myself there, afterwards,
right as rain that doesn't fall, doesn't
darken a perfect day. Our sweet
and gentle choreography
is a ballet of what is blessed.

I have no wish to compose you.
What I love is the way you are
never still, the way you fall
out of yourself and into me:
your gift of tulips in a pint glass;
still life; this cool bliss, fullness.

Interior Fictions

Like Flying

Last night he dreamt he was flying – fingers
winged with swimming, belly full of feathers.

Sky pulses warm air, like his mother's breath
in his hair, his face lifted in a smile.

He doesn't know why he stops there – that house –
but when he walks through the front door, his feet

don't touch the ground. From the light and dark
of the hall, doors close and open; stairs lead

somewhere else. Yellow. Listen. He can
hear the small music of mice in the skirting.

They are chewing his thoughts away, shredding
his memory to build their nests. He must

decide upon colour, shape, dimension.
He must turn his head like a bird, forage

for berries, crumbs. Every day he forgets
something old. Every day he remembers

something new: the pictures in his head, blurred
reflections, where his body thinks it's lived.

Like Falling

One day he meets her for the first time
and remembers his face reflected in her eyes.

Dandelion clocks. Brown-skinned summers.
The peeling walls get taller and taller

until, on tiptoe, the ceiling touches
the sky. And what he feels is falling –

gravity tugging the dumb corners
of his mouth, her saying the words he learnt

by heart. Soon they are eating strawberries
as if they grew on trees. They tumble down

the tunnel of sweet dark and bounce back. Look.
Feathers fly and fall like flakes of the moon

they don't even notice climbing through the crack
in the curtains. Till morning when every day

is another small death to sing. Such stillness.
The holding on and letting go that makes

pictures of our bodies when they're not there –
the warmth of a mattress, an empty glass.

ON THE GAME

Selling Yourself Short

The first is always the worst. Thank god
for the fog of alcohol. Afterwards

there wasn't enough water in the pipes
to wash away the dirt souring my skin.

I cleaned the house from top to bottom.
Still couldn't rinse the thought of it away.

Don't think I'm the only one snagged in the loop
of those big black lies: *easy money*;

just a job; don't worry, you're in control.
It's a state of mind you're out there selling

with the cold fact of your body, setting your watch
on the forty-minute hour, trying

to think about something else. Anything
but the game you're playing: him pretending

he isn't paying; you acting as if
you like it. When people used to ask

what I wanted to be when I grew up,
I never dreamed this might be the answer.

Working girl. On the game.
If you do it once, you become it.

You cut out the words you don't want to hear.
And every night is another first.

Accounting

If she traded in their hard currency,
she'd say sex is closer to death
than she'll ever let the johns get.
Though she'll do it without a second skin.
If they pay enough. If she's high enough.
A girl's got to keep herself. And love
doesn't come into it. She'll name her price,
see the colour of their money, make
a small killing she'll spend on crack.
And aren't the streets paved with it?

Just how old will she never own up to
when the man next door said to call
him *Uncle,* keep *their little secret?*
Behind the crack, a seven year old kid
shuts her eyes as the punter slams it in.
And her feet ache like fuck. On a good night,
a handful of blow-jobs in the back
of Japanese cars that make the sore
places at the sides of her mouth weep,
make her want to bite. But the crack
keeps her smiling. Who cares about dying?
She can't add up her life to much.

She drinks a lot of coffee. Four sugars.
On the streets at the end of a shift, thin,
hungover, she'll reckon she's a lucky tart,
with the luxury of a bed to fall into
and dream about her mother,
the colour of her eyes: moving pictures,
the words censored she can't afford.
One night will blur into another,
a few hours of daylight, the crack
between, the one thing that keeps her going.

...What I Know Now

Now I know they're all the same. A standing cock
has no conscience: punter, lover or pimp.

Now I know I was just kidding myself;
couldn't see the gold in his eyes
was my own light. Even after that night
he broke me in with a gang of his mates:
I should have run but I could hardly walk.
He said sorry, standing in my blind spot.

Now I know the way to a man's heart
is through his pocket. All there was left of me
were the bruises, the scars his knife etched
in my skin: his brand, our secret binding.
I looked in the mirror and saw a whore
waiting to be transformed into a dream princess.

Now I know the only way to get out
of it is to get out of it. But what's
crooked can never be straight. He's doing time
for setting a girl on fire. *Big Car Small Dick.*
He didn't laugh. That could have been me,
burnt like so much waste paper.

Now I know I'll never do it again
for anyone else. I am the star of my own story.
Cocaine's my ponce. That's all that gets me up
and on the streets. The twitches, the shakes, they don't
go away but I'm not in the business
of kidding myself, not anymore. Not now I know.

Sexual Politics

She is a woman who knows when a fuck
has zips. And this, sweetheart, is it. First mistake:

doing it for a dare, stars dripping
post-coitally down from an axis

of Acapulco Gold, Lebanese Black.
A man who plays a stringed instrument while cities

burn is not a man to turn down. At the
21 Club she will consider the implications

of espionage, black leather; realise she's a leper,
not about to change her spots; the S & M

kicks of Tory monogamy, a card she'll never carry.
The party will go on. Even though the bastards

always close ranks, caught with their trousers down,
another member exposed. They're all the same

in the dark. And it's there she locates
the brightest spark of hatred for everything

anyone's ever told her is good. She's
a conscientious abstainer who always says *yes*.

A girl's got to live. The judge's eyes are blue
as the skies in Florida. A pair of pink silk panties

are stitched inside his wig. She knows she wasn't
called Mandy for nothing; she'll never lie back

and think of England, men with names like Jack,
Stephen, Rachmann, something she can't remember

in Russian. She wishes when she never had it
so good, she could remember she didn't.

A week's a fucking long time.

The Mother

For she is all our mothers:
a vessel of glass containing the first
and the last, the intoxicating dark.
Her mystery is the historical DNA of sons.
When what's between her legs becomes
more interesting than she is, she's convinced
it's true; hides behind the glaze of her eyes,
the soft abandon of her thighs, white and vital,
as heroin smouldering over water.
She changes like a dream of geography,
greedy as a fish. Had she the decency to be
scientific, she'd be multiplication, the terror
of *more*. A four-letter word: subject and object
of confusion, requiring only the addition
of the verb *to fuck*. The limits of her body
are borderless countries laid waste over
and over. She is a world to be conquered,
a bed to lie in. Who will find it in his heart
to respect her when he knows she'll always
surrender? She does this out of love.
She makes every mother-fucking son feel like a king.
A penis needs no eye. What she offers
is an open door, the warmth inside, closing
like a trap; the tunnel inside her
that needs to be mined for the power inside her
so it explodes all over, becomes power *over* her.
Sometimes it's easier to let her think
she's doing the thinking. Save yourself the trouble.
She is trouble. Her impossible body,
her invisible orgasms, her flagrant blood.
The power inside her. Everything that's gorgeous,
she is, everything despicable. She is wanted.
She gives you heaven, gives you bloody hell.
Everyone's mother is a whore.
May she be wise.

In Kind

Such a gentleman, lowering black wool
on your shoulders, he bends to kiss the nest
of your neck, breathe in its dangerous scent.
Your white throat is wreathed with garlic jewels,
the empty cases of prawns. Then you know
you are to be his after-dinner mint,
his petit-four. Only your eyes say *no*
to what he's adding up. As if you count.

Pocketing his keys, he invites himself
in; needs the bite of black coffee before
skulking back to his wife, a mongrel home
from adventures. His braces stretch across
a three-course belly; five raw fingers
fork your crossed thigh. You know you want the prick
to leave; but he wants your share of the bill
he paid, insisting, *my dear*. His pleasure.

Your new settee's giving, getting smaller.
Acid vinaigrette curdles in your throat;
paella peppering your tongue. Heartburn:
a sour aftertaste. He unfolds your legs
like a napkin. Prefers it with the lights
on – the opposite of *no* – what he can't
have at home. You wake up alone, the bed
smelling of sweat, your own; the price of it.

Proposition

You've got something that he wants that gives you
the power he wants. And once the question's
asked how much can you resist? It stays
on your skin like an itch in a place
it's not polite to scratch. You scratch.

You imagine the protocol: no kissing,
no marks on the body, cash on the table.
The cool edge of the kitchen table
jamming its angle against your legs.
His breath. The punchline. The buckling up.
Three notes in the fruit bowl smelling
of someone else's hands. No one will see the marks.

You tell yourself it would be a favour,
a bargain, for a friend. Just a simple answer
to a simple question he'll never ask
again. But how poor, how sharp, how empty
must you be to know how much is enough?

Role Exchange: A Found Poem

I find a woman who has worked
as a professional prostitute
for ten years.
At this point I have also worked
as an artist for ten years.

I propose to exchange roles.
She accepts.

She replaces me at my opening
at De Appel Gallery in Amsterdam.
At the same time I sit in her place
in a window of the red light district.

We both take full responsibility
for our roles.

4 hrs. 1975. Marina Abramović.

Selling Oranges

The streets are rivers of filth and urchins; and me,
I pick up my skirts, my ankles, and step
from stone to stone. I keep myself
to myself, selling oranges to men in stinking wigs,
my body, bright despite the dark, a sharpness
I adore, catch in the air. But no stone
takes me to the right gate, the gate
with the key, the iron key stiff in the lock.

So I sell my bright oranges, dimpled
like their greasy buttocks. It makes me smile,
a banana I've never even seen. I look
in the mirror of their faces and see all
they want is to unpeel my yellow silks,
finger the lips of my lace. They address
my breasts, pink and white as marble,
frozen under their hot breath.

My only interest is the lump in their breeches,
the one that clinks like the gate of heaven;
that melts me. It's all I have, this living
hand to mouth, not knowing whose hand,
whose mouth. Every night is a different bed
and as long as there's a body by my side,
the dreams stay away, the dark. If I could,
I'd dream I was an owl trailing night sounds
in the air, a beautiful cloak behind me.

The Feckless Gypsy

(after Lorca)

So I took him down to the river
and told him I was a virgin.
It was obvious he was married.
It was the Feast of Magdalena.
I was only doing my job.
The streetlights went off
and the cicadas took over.
At the edge of the town
I touched his pigeon chest
and it sizzled
like plucked feathers.
His leather trousers
crackled in my ears
like a bull's hide
pierced by five spears.
No silver fringing their leaves,
the trees seemed taller.
A sky-line of stray dogs
howled in the distance.

Past the blackberry bushes,
the rushes, the hawthorn,
I carved a hollow for his head
in the sand.
I took off my blouse.
He took off his trousers.
I undid my belt.
He left his watch on.
The cheapest brandy was nothing
to his rancid skin.
He thought the sun
shone out of his arse.
His pelvis played
like a forgetful goldfish
in and out of a fountain.

That night I coasted
down an old road
in a clapped-out banger.
As a lady of the evening
I can't repeat what he said to me:
we have our rules.
All covered in sand and lipstick
I pulled him up from the riverbank.
Fingers of iris
clawed the air.

I acted like the woman I am,
a whore with a heart of gold;
I asked him to give me
whatever was most expensive,
satin the colour of straw.
I wasn't going to touch him again,
because though I wasn't a virgin,
he might as well have been,
that night I took him by the river.

French Letter

*Je m'appelle Isabelle. Je suis ta fille
de joie.* I feel more like Eurotunnel

when I pretend to be French and offer
them lessons. They want a Mademoiselle

like they want Burgundy or Brie. I wear
French knickers, mime French kisses; make my lips

pucker, my kitten eyes sulk. My business
is a bedroom farce – all those stupid men,

caught with their trousers down, pricks in the air
like little pink piglets rooting for truffles.

They have delusions of haute cuisine
while I dream of haute couture, moaning

in a French accent so they can feel
like Napoleon, and me, their empire.

I know they're short of French culture at home.
And something that good is even better

in a foreign language. They can almost
convince themselves it never happened.

Isn't guilt what the English are best at?
La joie est morte. Vive la joie.

Detective Love

We found the corpse of a Chinese woman
in the West End, scars like little crescents
of desire across her face, what was left
of her body.
                    Rewinding the story:
Soho Square Gardens, business, pleasure, *girls
wanted*, we discovered amber
was the resting place of a tiger's soul,
yellow resin glazed around time and courage.

City streets weren't paved with its absence
of geometry. Her small feet walking
the long way home were only waiting
for the scarlet storm to break; deep secrets,
a plot out of Shakespeare, or Louis L'Amour.
Look what happens when East meets West. Do larks
exult?
                    The tiger brooch with emerald eyes
told us China wouldn't be the last
woman to end up that way, cheek jagged
with the mark of the beast that says yes in
a language which is international.

In Soho they're hot on French culture.
Our English raincoats were getting dirty.

Nights back home with our good women
are whisky dreams reeking of sex
and death, insects trapped in amber.

The John Sonnets

1

I was too old for innocence, too young
for experience. There was no other way.

If not for the beer, I might not have done
anything about it. I seized the day
like a hound when one of the girls who stay
in the shadows outside the pub called out
to me. All that worrying what to say,
how to choose, and *she* chose *me*.
                              A blackout
where my brain should be. My white heart.
                                        Without
any emotion. Like having a crap.

But now I knew what it was all about
I could do it with real girls. I'd bought the map.

Like all animals, I felt a bit sad.
Never knew her name, the first one I had.

2

It all started out as a joke. A guy
from work bought me a session for Christmas.
Gift-wrapped.
              I was scared shitless. I'm quite shy
about sex but this girl was so dextrous
I was too excited to feel anxious.
So I got hooked. Four times a week. Lunch hours.
Evenings.
            I liked her to dress up. Luscious
in fishnets and stilettos, she'd devour
me. Do anything. I loved the power.
No hassles. The cash kept it clean.
                        Some nights
I'd stay over; send her a single flower
the next day.
            Ten years of this and no fights.

Until someone's big mouth changed my life.

And it isn't the same without a wife.

3

She used to like it.
             A sprinkle of salt
and pepper, a handful of extra pounds,
now everything's changed.
                 It's nobody's fault.
We talk carefully about nothing; sounds
drip like spittle from our lips.
                It's not grounds
for divorce. Just six years since we last kissed.

But I still want her so much it astounds
me. Enough to do it with a tart. Pissed
mostly so all I can see is a mist
where her face should be.
                                It's better that way:
no names.
              I try not to get in a twist
about the money. The kids. The price I pay.

I think of her, gripping a stranger's hips.
My eyes miss her eyes. My lips miss her lips.

4

The way I see it, it's one of the perks
of the job. Just an honest trade. Tax free.

Pick them up at the station. Lonely berks.
I fiddle the clock to double their fee.

We have an arrangement, the girl with curves
that make my engine burn and me:
                                    if she
is idling, I give her what she deserves.

Don't get me wrong. I'm not one of those pervs
into chains and stuff. There's just certain things
I couldn't ask the wife to do.
                                Her nerves
are bad.
          This way we're both happy.
                                    No strings.

Who'd want a wife who's common as muck?
There's one you love and the other you fuck.

5

When I go out to do a woman in
I always wear clean shoes and my good suit.

There's nothing that beats the glamour of sin.

I cover my tracks, take a different route
every time, for the public good, I shoot
my load inside some slut I don't know
and who doesn't know me.
                              They're better mute
so I gag them.
                  Then cut them up.
                                          I show
them who's in control. I take what they owe.

It's good to ruin someone else's day.

I just like to see how far I can go.
And if they die, nobody has to pay.

It's not their fault. It's their mothers I blame.

Don't you hate how women are all the same?

My Muse, the Whore

She is my right hand woman, my best friend. I know
I can only trust her as much as I trust myself.

She lounges around, pretending to be unavailable,
playing hide and seek, perfectly happy, smoking

better cigarettes than I can afford, fragrant, foreign,
filing her nails into french-polished almonds,

listening to women's voices on the radio, just
waiting for me to whistle. She's the best

lover I've ever had, the only one to deserve all
the attention she demands. Which I give freely,

our hands touching like the blue and yellow
of irises coupled in a tight-lipped vase, full

of sugar, or aspirin, to eke out their short time.
I pay her in American dollars, eagles. She never

complains; leaves me with the shape of a door,
a siphoned look about the eyes, skin crackling.

The way she strokes my palm makes me forget
the etiquette of dexterity, makes me surrender.

Our pulses are indigo streaks of lightning.
She whispers in my ear for more and more.

My left hand powders her cheek and thinks
of lilies, the taste of pollen on its five tongues.

I hear her laughing and it is an old sad song
I know the words to. She is an open book

with a marbled spine. I am the minder
of her scarlet heart. And I never tire

of listening to her stories, passing them on
like butterfly cakes in patterned paper cases.

We never use a microwave. Recharge the batteries
for our deluxe vibrator. What I like

about her is how she makes jokes
and doesn't care if nobody laughs. She isn't scared

to cry. We go back a long way, old friends
with a history that never dies. Always another trick.